BABY
LOG BOOK

Baby's name:
_____

Baby Log Book

Date

eat schedule

TIME	FOOD	AMOUNT

sleep schedule

FROM	TO	TOTAL TIME

Activities

baby

Notes

....
....
....
....
....

Shopping list

Diapers

Time	Pee	Poop
....	☐	☐
....	☐	☐
....	☐	☐
....	☐	☐
....	☐	☐
....	☐	☐
....	☐	☐
....	☐	☐

Baby Log Book

Date

eat schedule

TIME	FOOD	AMOUNT

sleep schedule

FROM	TO	TOTAL TIME

Activities

baby

Notes

....
....
....
....
....

Shopping list

Diapers

Time	Pee	Poop
......	☐	☐
......	☐	☐
......	☐	☐
......	☐	☐
......	☐	☐
......	☐	☐
......	☐	☐
......	☐	☐

Baby Log Book

Date

eat schedule

TIME	FOOD	AMOUNT

sleep schedule

FROM	TO	TOTAL TIME

Activities

baby

Notes

Diapers

Time	Pee	Poop
......	☐	☐
......	☐	☐
......	☐	☐
......	☐	☐
......	☐	☐
......	☐	☐
......	☐	☐
......	☐	☐

Shopping list

Baby Log Book — Date

eat schedule

TIME	FOOD	AMOUNT

sleep schedule

FROM	TO	TOTAL TIME

Activities

baby

Notes

....
....
....
....
....

Shopping list

Diapers

Time	Pee	Poop
......	☐	☐
......	☐	☐
......	☐	☐
......	☐	☐
......	☐	☐
......	☐	☐
......	☐	☐
......	☐	☐

Baby Log Book — Date

eat schedule

TIME	FOOD	AMOUNT

sleep schedule

FROM	TO	TOTAL TIME

Activities

baby

Notes

....
....
....
....
....

Shopping list

Diapers

Time	Pee	Poop
……	☐	☐
……	☐	☐
……	☐	☐
……	☐	☐
……	☐	☐
……	☐	☐
……	☐	☐
……	☐	☐

Baby Log Book

Date

eat schedule

TIME	FOOD	AMOUNT

sleep schedule

FROM	TO	TOTAL TIME

Activities

baby

Notes

....
....
....
....
....

Shopping list

Diapers

Time	Pee	Poop
......	☐	☐
......	☐	☐
......	☐	☐
......	☐	☐
......	☐	☐
......	☐	☐
......	☐	☐
......	☐	☐

Baby Log Book   Date

eat schedule

TIME	FOOD	AMOUNT

sleep schedule

FROM	TO	TOTAL TIME

Activities

baby

Notes

....
....
....
....
....

Shopping list

Diapers

Time	Pee	Poop
......	☐	☐
......	☐	☐
......	☐	☐
......	☐	☐
......	☐	☐
......	☐	☐
......	☐	☐
......	☐	☐

Baby Log Book　Date

eat schedule

TIME	FOOD	AMOUNT

sleep schedule

FROM	TO	TOTAL TIME

Activities

baby

Notes

....
....
....
....
....

Shopping list

Diapers

Time	Pee	Poop
....	☐	☐
....	☐	☐
....	☐	☐
....	☐	☐
....	☐	☐
....	☐	☐
....	☐	☐
....	☐	☐

Baby Log Book

Date

eat schedule

TIME	FOOD	AMOUNT

sleep schedule

FROM	TO	TOTAL TIME

Activities

baby

Notes

....
....
....
....
....

Shopping list

Diapers

Time	Pee	Poop
....	☐	☐
....	☐	☐
....	☐	☐
....	☐	☐
....	☐	☐
....	☐	☐
....	☐	☐
....	☐	☐

Baby Log Book Date

eat schedule

TIME	FOOD	AMOUNT

sleep schedule

FROM	TO	TOTAL TIME

Activities

baby

Notes

....
....
....
....
....

Shopping list

Diapers

Time	Pee	Poop
......	☐	☐
......	☐	☐
......	☐	☐
......	☐	☐
......	☐	☐
......	☐	☐
......	☐	☐
......	☐	☐

Baby Log Book Date

eat schedule

TIME	FOOD	AMOUNT

sleep schedule

FROM	TO	TOTAL TIME

Activities

baby

Notes

....
....
....
....
....

Shopping list

Diapers

Time	Pee	Poop
.....	☐	☐
.....	☐	☐
.....	☐	☐
.....	☐	☐
.....	☐	☐
.....	☐	☐
.....	☐	☐
.....	☐	☐

Baby Log Book   Date

eat schedule

TIME	FOOD	AMOUNT

sleep schedule

FROM	TO	TOTAL TIME

Activities

baby

Notes

....
....
....
....
....

Shopping list

Diapers

Time	Pee	Poop
....	☐	☐
....	☐	☐
....	☐	☐
....	☐	☐
....	☐	☐
....	☐	☐
....	☐	☐
....	☐	☐

Baby Log Book

Date

eat schedule

TIME	FOOD	AMOUNT

sleep schedule

FROM	TO	TOTAL TIME

Activities

baby

Notes

....
....
....
....
....

Shopping list

Diapers

Time	Pee	Poop
....	☐	☐
....	☐	☐
....	☐	☐
....	☐	☐
....	☐	☐
....	☐	☐
....	☐	☐
....	☐	☐

Baby Log Book   Date

eat schedule

TIME	FOOD	AMOUNT

sleep schedule

FROM	TO	TOTAL TIME

Activities

baby

Notes

....
....
....
....
....

Shopping list

Diapers

Time	Pee	Poop
......	☐	☐
......	☐	☐
......	☐	☐
......	☐	☐
......	☐	☐
......	☐	☐
......	☐	☐
......	☐	☐

Baby Log Book Date

eat schedule

TIME	FOOD	AMOUNT

sleep schedule

FROM	TO	TOTAL TIME

Activities

baby

Notes

....
....
....
....
....

Shopping list

Diapers

Time	Pee	Poop
......	☐	☐
......	☐	☐
......	☐	☐
......	☐	☐
......	☐	☐
......	☐	☐
......	☐	☐
......	☐	☐

Baby Log Book Date

eat schedule

TIME	FOOD	AMOUNT

sleep schedule

FROM	TO	TOTAL TIME

Activities

baby

Notes

....
....
....
....
....

Shopping list

Diapers

Time	Pee	Poop
.....	☐	☐
.....	☐	☐
.....	☐	☐
.....	☐	☐
.....	☐	☐
.....	☐	☐
.....	☐	☐
.....	☐	☐

Baby Log Book Date

eat schedule

TIME	FOOD	AMOUNT

sleep schedule

FROM	TO	TOTAL TIME

Activities

baby

Notes

....
....
....
....
....

Shopping list

Diapers

Time	Pee	Poop
......	☐	☐
......	☐	☐
......	☐	☐
......	☐	☐
......	☐	☐
......	☐	☐
......	☐	☐
......	☐	☐

Baby Log Book

Date

eat schedule

TIME	FOOD	AMOUNT

sleep schedule

FROM	TO	TOTAL TIME

Activities

baby

Notes

....
....
....
....
....

Shopping list

Diapers

Time	Pee	Poop
.....	☐	☐
.....	☐	☐
.....	☐	☐
.....	☐	☐
.....	☐	☐
.....	☐	☐
.....	☐	☐
.....	☐	☐

Baby Log Book   Date

eat schedule

TIME	FOOD	AMOUNT

sleep schedule

FROM	TO	TOTAL TIME

Activities

baby

Notes

....
....
....
....

Shopping list

Diapers

Time	Pee	Poop
......	☐	☐
......	☐	☐
......	☐	☐
......	☐	☐
......	☐	☐
......	☐	☐
......	☐	☐
......	☐	☐

Baby Log Book

Date

eat schedule

TIME	FOOD	AMOUNT

sleep schedule

FROM	TO	TOTAL TIME

Activities

baby

Notes

....
....
....
....
....

Shopping list

Diapers

Time	Pee	Poop
......	☐	☐
......	☐	☐
......	☐	☐
......	☐	☐
......	☐	☐
......	☐	☐
......	☐	☐
......	☐	☐

Baby Log Book   Date

eat schedule

TIME	FOOD	AMOUNT

sleep schedule

FROM	TO	TOTAL TIME

Activities

baby

Notes

....
....
....
....
....

Diapers

Time	Pee	Poop
………	☐	☐
………	☐	☐
………	☐	☐
………	☐	☐
………	☐	☐
………	☐	☐
………	☐	☐
………	☐	☐

Shopping list

Baby Log Book

Date

eat schedule

TIME	FOOD	AMOUNT

sleep schedule

FROM	TO	TOTAL TIME

Activities

baby

Notes

....
....
....
....
....

Shopping list

Diapers

Time	Pee	Poop
.....	☐	☐
.....	☐	☐
.....	☐	☐
.....	☐	☐
.....	☐	☐
.....	☐	☐
.....	☐	☐
.....	☐	☐

Baby Log Book

Date

eat schedule

TIME	FOOD	AMOUNT

sleep schedule

FROM	TO	TOTAL TIME

Activities

baby

Notes

....
....
....
....
....

Shopping list

Diapers

Time	Pee	Poop
.....	☐	☐
.....	☐	☐
.....	☐	☐
.....	☐	☐
.....	☐	☐
.....	☐	☐
.....	☐	☐
.....	☐	☐

Baby Log Book — Date

eat schedule

TIME	FOOD	AMOUNT

sleep schedule

FROM	TO	TOTAL TIME

Activities

baby

Notes

....
....
....
....
....

Shopping list

Diapers

Time	Pee	Poop
......	☐	☐
......	☐	☐
......	☐	☐
......	☐	☐
......	☐	☐
......	☐	☐
......	☐	☐
......	☐	☐

Baby Log Book

Date

eat schedule

TIME	FOOD	AMOUNT

sleep schedule

FROM	TO	TOTAL TIME

Activities

baby

Notes

....
....
....
....
....

Shopping list

Diapers

Time	Pee	Poop
......	☐	☐
......	☐	☐
......	☐	☐
......	☐	☐
......	☐	☐
......	☐	☐
......	☐	☐
......	☐	☐

Baby Log Book

Date

eat schedule

TIME	FOOD	AMOUNT

sleep schedule

FROM	TO	TOTAL TIME

Activities

baby

Notes

....
....
....
....
....

Shopping list

Diapers

Time	Pee	Poop
......	☐	☐
......	☐	☐
......	☐	☐
......	☐	☐
......	☐	☐
......	☐	☐
......	☐	☐
......	☐	☐

Baby Log Book Date

eat schedule

TIME	FOOD	AMOUNT

sleep schedule

FROM	TO	TOTAL TIME

Activities

baby

Notes

....
....
....
....
....

Shopping list

Diapers

Time	Pee	Poop
......	☐	☐
......	☐	☐
......	☐	☐
......	☐	☐
......	☐	☐
......	☐	☐
......	☐	☐
......	☐	☐

Baby Log Book

Date

eat schedule

TIME	FOOD	AMOUNT

sleep schedule

FROM	TO	TOTAL TIME

Activities

baby

Notes

....
....
....
....
....

Shopping list

Diapers

Time	Pee	Poop
.....	☐	☐
.....	☐	☐
.....	☐	☐
.....	☐	☐
.....	☐	☐
.....	☐	☐
.....	☐	☐
.....	☐	☐

Baby Log Book   Date

eat schedule

TIME	FOOD	AMOUNT

sleep schedule

FROM	TO	TOTAL TIME

Activities

baby

Notes

....
....
....
....
....

Shopping list

Diapers

Time	Pee	Poop
......	☐	☐
......	☐	☐
......	☐	☐
......	☐	☐
......	☐	☐
......	☐	☐
......	☐	☐
......	☐	☐

Baby Log Book Date

eat schedule

TIME	FOOD	AMOUNT

sleep schedule

FROM	TO	TOTAL TIME

Activities

baby

Notes

....
....
....
....
....

Shopping list

Diapers

Time	Pee	Poop
.....	☐	☐
.....	☐	☐
.....	☐	☐
.....	☐	☐
.....	☐	☐
.....	☐	☐
.....	☐	☐
.....	☐	☐

Baby Log Book Date

eat schedule

TIME	FOOD	AMOUNT

sleep schedule

FROM	TO	TOTAL TIME

Activities

baby

Notes

....
....
....
....
....

Shopping list

Diapers

Time	Pee	Poop
....	☐	☐
....	☐	☐
....	☐	☐
....	☐	☐
....	☐	☐
....	☐	☐
....	☐	☐
....	☐	☐

Baby Log Book — Date

eat schedule

TIME	FOOD	AMOUNT

sleep schedule

FROM	TO	TOTAL TIME

Activities

baby

Notes

....
....
....
....
....

Shopping list

Diapers

Time	Pee	Poop
......	☐	☐
......	☐	☐
......	☐	☐
......	☐	☐
......	☐	☐
......	☐	☐
......	☐	☐
......	☐	☐

Baby Log Book

Date

eat schedule

TIME	FOOD	AMOUNT

sleep schedule

FROM	TO	TOTAL TIME

Activities

baby

Notes

....
....
....
....
....

Shopping list

Diapers

Time	Pee	Poop
......	☐	☐
......	☐	☐
......	☐	☐
......	☐	☐
......	☐	☐
......	☐	☐
......	☐	☐
......	☐	☐

Baby Log Book

Date

eat schedule

TIME	FOOD	AMOUNT

sleep schedule

FROM	TO	TOTAL TIME

Activities

baby

Notes

....
....
....
....
....

Shopping list

Diapers

Time	Pee	Poop
......	☐	☐
......	☐	☐
......	☐	☐
......	☐	☐
......	☐	☐
......	☐	☐
......	☐	☐
......	☐	☐

Baby Log Book   Date

eat schedule

TIME	FOOD	AMOUNT

sleep schedule

FROM	TO	TOTAL TIME

Activities

baby

Notes

....
....
....
....
....

Shopping list

Diapers

Time	Pee	Poop
......	☐	☐
......	☐	☐
......	☐	☐
......	☐	☐
......	☐	☐
......	☐	☐
......	☐	☐
......	☐	☐

Baby Log Book

Date

eat schedule

TIME	FOOD	AMOUNT

sleep schedule

FROM	TO	TOTAL TIME

Activities

baby

Notes

....
....
....
....
....

Shopping list

Diapers

Time	Pee	Poop
.....	☐	☐
.....	☐	☐
.....	☐	☐
.....	☐	☐
.....	☐	☐
.....	☐	☐
.....	☐	☐
.....	☐	☐

Baby Log Book

Date

eat schedule

TIME	FOOD	AMOUNT

sleep schedule

FROM	TO	TOTAL TIME

Activities

baby

Notes

....
....
....
....
....

Shopping list

Diapers

Time	Pee	Poop
......	☐	☐
......	☐	☐
......	☐	☐
......	☐	☐
......	☐	☐
......	☐	☐
......	☐	☐
......	☐	☐

Baby Log Book Date

eat schedule

TIME	FOOD	AMOUNT

sleep schedule

FROM	TO	TOTAL TIME

Activities

baby

Notes

....
....
....
....
....

Shopping list

Diapers

Time	Pee	Poop
.....	☐	☐
.....	☐	☐
.....	☐	☐
.....	☐	☐
.....	☐	☐
.....	☐	☐
.....	☐	☐
.....	☐	☐

Baby Log Book — Date

eat schedule

TIME	FOOD	AMOUNT

sleep schedule

FROM	TO	TOTAL TIME

Activities

baby

Notes

....
....
....
....
....

Shopping list

Diapers

Time	Pee	Poop
......	☐	☐
......	☐	☐
......	☐	☐
......	☐	☐
......	☐	☐
......	☐	☐
......	☐	☐
......	☐	☐

Baby Log Book   Date

eat schedule

TIME	FOOD	AMOUNT

sleep schedule

FROM	TO	TOTAL TIME

Activities

baby

Notes

....
....
....
....
....

Diapers

Time	Pee	Poop
.....	☐	☐
.....	☐	☐
.....	☐	☐
.....	☐	☐
.....	☐	☐
.....	☐	☐
.....	☐	☐
.....	☐	☐

Shopping list

Baby Log Book   Date

eat schedule

TIME	FOOD	AMOUNT

sleep schedule

FROM	TO	TOTAL TIME

Activities

baby

Notes

....
....
....
....
....

Shopping list

Diapers

Time	Pee	Poop
......	☐	☐
......	☐	☐
......	☐	☐
......	☐	☐
......	☐	☐
......	☐	☐
......	☐	☐
......	☐	☐

Baby Log Book   Date

eat schedule

TIME	FOOD	AMOUNT

sleep schedule

FROM	TO	TOTAL TIME

Activities

baby

Notes

....
....
....
....
....

Shopping list

Diapers

Time	Pee	Poop
......	☐	☐
......	☐	☐
......	☐	☐
......	☐	☐
......	☐	☐
......	☐	☐
......	☐	☐
......	☐	☐

Baby Log Book

Date

eat schedule

TIME	FOOD	AMOUNT

sleep schedule

FROM	TO	TOTAL TIME

Activities

baby

Notes

....
....
....
....
....

Shopping list

Diapers

Time	Pee	Poop
......	☐	☐
......	☐	☐
......	☐	☐
......	☐	☐
......	☐	☐
......	☐	☐
......	☐	☐
......	☐	☐
......	☐	☐

Baby Log Book Date

eat schedule

TIME	FOOD	AMOUNT

sleep schedule

FROM	TO	TOTAL TIME

Activities

baby

Notes

....
....
....
....
....

Diapers

Time	Pee	Poop
......	☐	☐
......	☐	☐
......	☐	☐
......	☐	☐
......	☐	☐
......	☐	☐
......	☐	☐
......	☐	☐

Shopping list

Baby Log Book Date

eat schedule

TIME	FOOD	AMOUNT

sleep schedule

FROM	TO	TOTAL TIME

Activities

baby

Notes

....
....
....
....
....

Shopping list

Diapers

Time	Pee	Poop
....	☐	☐
....	☐	☐
....	☐	☐
....	☐	☐
....	☐	☐
....	☐	☐
....	☐	☐
....	☐	☐

Baby Log Book   Date

eat schedule

TIME	FOOD	AMOUNT

sleep schedule

FROM	TO	TOTAL TIME

Activities

baby

Notes

....
....
....
....
....

Shopping list

Diapers

Time	Pee	Poop
.....	☐	☐
.....	☐	☐
.....	☐	☐
.....	☐	☐
.....	☐	☐
.....	☐	☐
.....	☐	☐
.....	☐	☐

Baby Log Book   Date

eat schedule

TIME	FOOD	AMOUNT

sleep schedule

FROM	TO	TOTAL TIME

Activities

baby

Notes

....
....
....
....
....

Shopping list

Diapers

Time	Pee	Poop
……	☐	☐
……	☐	☐
……	☐	☐
……	☐	☐
……	☐	☐
……	☐	☐
……	☐	☐
……	☐	☐

Baby Log Book

Date

eat schedule

TIME	FOOD	AMOUNT

sleep schedule

FROM	TO	TOTAL TIME

Activities

baby

Notes

....
....
....
....
....

Shopping list

Diapers

Time	Pee	Poop
……	☐	☐
……	☐	☐
……	☐	☐
……	☐	☐
……	☐	☐
……	☐	☐
……	☐	☐
……	☐	☐

Baby Log Book

Date

eat schedule

TIME	FOOD	AMOUNT

sleep schedule

FROM	TO	TOTAL TIME

Activities

baby

Notes

....
....
....
....
....

Shopping list

Diapers

Time	Pee	Poop
......	☐	☐
......	☐	☐
......	☐	☐
......	☐	☐
......	☐	☐
......	☐	☐
......	☐	☐
......	☐	☐

Baby Log Book   Date

eat schedule

TIME	FOOD	AMOUNT

sleep schedule

FROM	TO	TOTAL TIME

Activities

baby

Notes

....
....
....
....
....

Shopping list

Diapers

Time	Pee	Poop
......	☐	☐
......	☐	☐
......	☐	☐
......	☐	☐
......	☐	☐
......	☐	☐
......	☐	☐
......	☐	☐

Baby Log Book   Date

eat schedule

TIME	FOOD	AMOUNT

sleep schedule

FROM	TO	TOTAL TIME

Activities

baby

Notes

....
....
....
....
....

Shopping list

Diapers

Time	Pee	Poop
......	☐	☐
......	☐	☐
......	☐	☐
......	☐	☐
......	☐	☐
......	☐	☐
......	☐	☐
......	☐	☐

Baby Log Book — Date

eat schedule

TIME	FOOD	AMOUNT

sleep schedule

FROM	TO	TOTAL TIME

Activities

baby

Notes

....
....
....
....
....

Shopping list

Diapers

Time	Pee	Poop
......	☐	☐
......	☐	☐
......	☐	☐
......	☐	☐
......	☐	☐
......	☐	☐
......	☐	☐
......	☐	☐

Baby Log Book   Date

eat schedule

TIME	FOOD	AMOUNT

sleep schedule

FROM	TO	TOTAL TIME

Activities

baby

Notes

....
....
....
....
....

Shopping list

Diapers

Time	Pee	Poop
....	☐	☐
....	☐	☐
....	☐	☐
....	☐	☐
....	☐	☐
....	☐	☐
....	☐	☐
....	☐	☐

Baby Log Book

Date

eat schedule

TIME	FOOD	AMOUNT

sleep schedule

FROM	TO	TOTAL TIME

Activities

baby

Notes

....
....
....
....
....

Shopping list

Diapers

Time	Pee	Poop
....	☐	☐
....	☐	☐
....	☐	☐
....	☐	☐
....	☐	☐
....	☐	☐
....	☐	☐
....	☐	☐

Baby Log Book

Date

eat schedule

TIME	FOOD	AMOUNT

sleep schedule

FROM	TO	TOTAL TIME

Activities

baby

Notes

....
....
....
....
....

Shopping list

Diapers

Time	Pee	Poop
.....	☐	☐
.....	☐	☐
.....	☐	☐
.....	☐	☐
.....	☐	☐
.....	☐	☐
.....	☐	☐
.....	☐	☐

Baby Log Book — Date

eat schedule

TIME	FOOD	AMOUNT

sleep schedule

FROM	TO	TOTAL TIME

Activities

baby

Notes

....
....
....
....
....

Shopping list

Diapers

Time	Pee	Poop
....	☐	☐
....	☐	☐
....	☐	☐
....	☐	☐
....	☐	☐
....	☐	☐
....	☐	☐
....	☐	☐

Baby Log Book

Date

eat schedule

TIME	FOOD	AMOUNT

sleep schedule

FROM	TO	TOTAL TIME

Activities

baby

Notes

....
....
....
....
....

Diapers

Time	Pee	Poop
......	☐	☐
......	☐	☐
......	☐	☐
......	☐	☐
......	☐	☐
......	☐	☐
......	☐	☐
......	☐	☐

Shopping list

Baby Log Book

Date

eat schedule

TIME	FOOD	AMOUNT

sleep schedule

FROM	TO	TOTAL TIME

Activities

baby

Notes

....
....
....
....
....

Shopping list

Diapers

Time	Pee	Poop
.....	☐	☐
.....	☐	☐
.....	☐	☐
.....	☐	☐
.....	☐	☐
.....	☐	☐
.....	☐	☐
.....	☐	☐

Baby Log Book — Date

eat schedule

TIME	FOOD	AMOUNT

sleep schedule

FROM	TO	TOTAL TIME

Activities

baby

Notes

....
....
....
....
....

Shopping list

Diapers

Time	Pee	Poop
……	☐	☐
……	☐	☐
……	☐	☐
……	☐	☐
……	☐	☐
……	☐	☐
……	☐	☐
……	☐	☐

Baby Log Book   Date

eat schedule

TIME	FOOD	AMOUNT

sleep schedule

FROM	TO	TOTAL TIME

Activities

baby

Notes

....
....
....
....
....

Shopping list

Diapers

Time	Pee	Poop
.....	☐	☐
.....	☐	☐
.....	☐	☐
.....	☐	☐
.....	☐	☐
.....	☐	☐
.....	☐	☐
.....	☐	☐

Baby Log Book   Date

eat schedule

TIME	FOOD	AMOUNT

sleep schedule

FROM	TO	TOTAL TIME

Activities

baby

Notes

....
....
....
....
....

Diapers

Time	Pee	Poop
......	☐	☐
......	☐	☐
......	☐	☐
......	☐	☐
......	☐	☐
......	☐	☐
......	☐	☐
......	☐	☐

Shopping list

Baby Log Book

Date

eat schedule

TIME	FOOD	AMOUNT

sleep schedule

FROM	TO	TOTAL TIME

Activities

baby

Notes

....
....
....
....
....

Shopping list

Diapers

Time Pee Poop
...... ☐ ☐
...... ☐ ☐
...... ☐ ☐
...... ☐ ☐
...... ☐ ☐
...... ☐ ☐
...... ☐ ☐
...... ☐ ☐

Baby Log Book Date

eat schedule

TIME	FOOD	AMOUNT

sleep schedule

FROM	TO	TOTAL TIME

Activities

baby

Notes

....
....
....
....
....

Shopping list

Diapers

Time	Pee	Poop
……	☐	☐
……	☐	☐
……	☐	☐
……	☐	☐
……	☐	☐
……	☐	☐
……	☐	☐
……	☐	☐

Baby Log Book — Date

eat schedule

TIME	FOOD	AMOUNT

sleep schedule

FROM	TO	TOTAL TIME

Activities

baby

Notes

....
....
....
....
....

Shopping list

Diapers

Time	Pee	Poop
....	☐	☐
....	☐	☐
....	☐	☐
....	☐	☐
....	☐	☐
....	☐	☐
....	☐	☐
....	☐	☐

Baby Log Book Date

eat schedule

TIME	FOOD	AMOUNT

sleep schedule

FROM	TO	TOTAL TIME

Activities

baby

Notes

....
....
....
....
....

Shopping list

Diapers

Time	Pee	Poop
......	☐	☐
......	☐	☐
......	☐	☐
......	☐	☐
......	☐	☐
......	☐	☐
......	☐	☐
......	☐	☐

Baby Log Book — Date

eat schedule

TIME	FOOD	AMOUNT

sleep schedule

FROM	TO	TOTAL TIME

Activities

baby

Notes

....
....
....
....
....

Shopping list

Diapers

Time	Pee	Poop
......	☐	☐
......	☐	☐
......	☐	☐
......	☐	☐
......	☐	☐
......	☐	☐
......	☐	☐
......	☐	☐

Baby Log Book Date

eat schedule

TIME	FOOD	AMOUNT

sleep schedule

FROM	TO	TOTAL TIME

Activities

baby

Notes

....
....
....
....

Shopping list

Diapers

Time	Pee	Poop
......	☐	☐
......	☐	☐
......	☐	☐
......	☐	☐
......	☐	☐
......	☐	☐
......	☐	☐
......	☐	☐

Baby Log Book   Date

eat schedule

TIME	FOOD	AMOUNT

sleep schedule

FROM	TO	TOTAL TIME

Activities

baby

Notes

Diapers

Time   Pee   Poop

Shopping list

Baby Log Book Date

eat schedule

TIME	FOOD	AMOUNT

sleep schedule

FROM	TO	TOTAL TIME

Activities

baby

Notes

....
....
....
....
....

Shopping list

Diapers

Time	Pee	Poop
......	☐	☐
......	☐	☐
......	☐	☐
......	☐	☐
......	☐	☐
......	☐	☐
......	☐	☐
......	☐	☐

Baby Log Book

Date

eat schedule

TIME	FOOD	AMOUNT

sleep schedule

FROM	TO	TOTAL TIME

Activities

baby

Notes

....
....
....
....
....

Shopping list

Diapers

Time	Pee	Poop
.....	☐	☐
.....	☐	☐
.....	☐	☐
.....	☐	☐
.....	☐	☐
.....	☐	☐
.....	☐	☐
.....	☐	☐

Baby Log Book   Date

eat schedule

TIME	FOOD	AMOUNT

sleep schedule

FROM	TO	TOTAL TIME

Activities

baby

Notes

....
....
....
....
....

Shopping list

Diapers

Time	Pee	Poop
......	☐	☐
......	☐	☐
......	☐	☐
......	☐	☐
......	☐	☐
......	☐	☐
......	☐	☐
......	☐	☐

Baby Log Book Date

eat schedule

TIME	FOOD	AMOUNT

sleep schedule

FROM	TO	TOTAL TIME

Activities

baby

Notes

....
....
....
....
....

Shopping list

Diapers

Time	Pee	Poop
......	☐	☐
......	☐	☐
......	☐	☐
......	☐	☐
......	☐	☐
......	☐	☐
......	☐	☐
......	☐	☐

Baby Log Book Date

eat schedule

TIME	FOOD	AMOUNT

sleep schedule

FROM	TO	TOTAL TIME

Activities

baby

Notes

....
....
....
....
....

Shopping list

Diapers

Time	Pee	Poop
......	☐	☐
......	☐	☐
......	☐	☐
......	☐	☐
......	☐	☐
......	☐	☐
......	☐	☐
......	☐	☐

Baby Log Book Date

eat schedule

TIME	FOOD	AMOUNT

sleep schedule

FROM	TO	TOTAL TIME

Activities

baby

Notes

....
....
....
....
....

Shopping list

Diapers

Time	Pee	Poop
......	☐	☐
......	☐	☐
......	☐	☐
......	☐	☐
......	☐	☐
......	☐	☐
......	☐	☐
......	☐	☐

Baby Log Book   Date

eat schedule

TIME	FOOD	AMOUNT

sleep schedule

FROM	TO	TOTAL TIME

Activities

baby

Notes

....

....

....

....

Diapers

Time	Pee	Poop
......	☐	☐
......	☐	☐
......	☐	☐
......	☐	☐
......	☐	☐
......	☐	☐
......	☐	☐
......	☐	☐

Shopping list

Baby Log Book

Date

eat schedule

TIME	FOOD	AMOUNT

sleep schedule

FROM	TO	TOTAL TIME

Activities

baby

Notes

....
....
....
....
....

Shopping list

Diapers

Time Pee Poop

…… ☐ ☐
…… ☐ ☐
…… ☐ ☐
…… ☐ ☐
…… ☐ ☐
…… ☐ ☐
…… ☐ ☐
…… ☐ ☐

Baby Log Book

Date

eat schedule

TIME	FOOD	AMOUNT

sleep schedule

FROM	TO	TOTAL TIME

Activities

baby

Notes

....
....
....
....
....

Shopping list

Diapers

Time	Pee	Poop
……	☐	☐
……	☐	☐
……	☐	☐
……	☐	☐
……	☐	☐
……	☐	☐
……	☐	☐
……	☐	☐

Baby Log Book Date

eat schedule

TIME	FOOD	AMOUNT

sleep schedule

FROM	TO	TOTAL TIME

Activities

baby

Notes

....
....
....
....
....

Shopping list

Diapers

Time	Pee	Poop
.....	☐	☐
.....	☐	☐
.....	☐	☐
.....	☐	☐
.....	☐	☐
.....	☐	☐
.....	☐	☐
.....	☐	☐

Baby Log Book Date

eat schedule

TIME	FOOD	AMOUNT

sleep schedule

FROM	TO	TOTAL TIME

Activities

baby

Notes

....
....
....
....
....

Shopping list

Diapers

Time	Pee	Poop
......	☐	☐
......	☐	☐
......	☐	☐
......	☐	☐
......	☐	☐
......	☐	☐
......	☐	☐
......	☐	☐

Baby Log Book Date

eat schedule

TIME	FOOD	AMOUNT

sleep schedule

FROM	TO	TOTAL TIME

Activities

baby

Notes

....
....
....
....
....

Shopping list

Diapers

Time	Pee	Poop
......	☐	☐
......	☐	☐
......	☐	☐
......	☐	☐
......	☐	☐
......	☐	☐
......	☐	☐
......	☐	☐

Baby Log Book

Date

eat schedule

TIME	FOOD	AMOUNT

sleep schedule

FROM	TO	TOTAL TIME

Activities

baby

Notes

....
....
....
....
....

Shopping list

Diapers

Time	Pee	Poop
......	☐	☐
......	☐	☐
......	☐	☐
......	☐	☐
......	☐	☐
......	☐	☐
......	☐	☐
......	☐	☐

Baby Log Book   Date

eat schedule

TIME	FOOD	AMOUNT

sleep schedule

FROM	TO	TOTAL TIME

Activities

baby

Notes

....
....
....
....
....

Shopping list

Diapers

Time	Pee	Poop
......	☐	☐
......	☐	☐
......	☐	☐
......	☐	☐
......	☐	☐
......	☐	☐
......	☐	☐
......	☐	☐

Baby Log Book

Date

eat schedule

TIME	FOOD	AMOUNT

sleep schedule

FROM	TO	TOTAL TIME

Activities

baby

Notes

....
....
....
....
....

Shopping list

Diapers

Time	Pee	Poop
……	☐	☐
……	☐	☐
……	☐	☐
……	☐	☐
……	☐	☐
……	☐	☐
……	☐	☐
……	☐	☐

Baby Log Book   Date

eat schedule

TIME	FOOD	AMOUNT

sleep schedule

FROM	TO	TOTAL TIME

Activities

baby

Notes

....
....
....
....
....

Shopping list

Diapers

Time	Pee	Poop
......	☐	☐
......	☐	☐
......	☐	☐
......	☐	☐
......	☐	☐
......	☐	☐
......	☐	☐
......	☐	☐

Baby Log Book

Date

eat schedule

TIME	FOOD	AMOUNT

sleep schedule

FROM	TO	TOTAL TIME

Activities

baby

Notes

....
....
....
....
....

Shopping list

Diapers

Time	Pee	Poop
......	☐	☐
......	☐	☐
......	☐	☐
......	☐	☐
......	☐	☐
......	☐	☐
......	☐	☐
......	☐	☐

Baby Log Book — Date

eat schedule

TIME	FOOD	AMOUNT

sleep schedule

FROM	TO	TOTAL TIME

Activities

baby

Notes

....
....
....
....
....

Shopping list

Diapers

Time	Pee	Poop
……	☐	☐
……	☐	☐
……	☐	☐
……	☐	☐
……	☐	☐
……	☐	☐
……	☐	☐
……	☐	☐

Baby Log Book

Date

eat schedule

TIME	FOOD	AMOUNT

sleep schedule

FROM	TO	TOTAL TIME

Activities

baby

Notes

....
....
....
....
....

Shopping list

Diapers

Time	Pee	Poop
.....	☐	☐
.....	☐	☐
.....	☐	☐
.....	☐	☐
.....	☐	☐
.....	☐	☐
.....	☐	☐
.....	☐	☐

Baby Log Book — Date

eat schedule

TIME	FOOD	AMOUNT

sleep schedule

FROM	TO	TOTAL TIME

Activities

baby

Notes

....
....
....
....
....

Shopping list

Diapers

Time	Pee	Poop
......	☐	☐
......	☐	☐
......	☐	☐
......	☐	☐
......	☐	☐
......	☐	☐
......	☐	☐
......	☐	☐

Baby Log Book   Date

eat schedule

TIME	FOOD	AMOUNT

sleep schedule

FROM	TO	TOTAL TIME

Activities

baby

Notes

....
....
....
....
....

Shopping list

Diapers

Time	Pee	Poop
.....	☐	☐
.....	☐	☐
.....	☐	☐
.....	☐	☐
.....	☐	☐
.....	☐	☐
.....	☐	☐
.....	☐	☐

Baby Log Book   Date

eat schedule

TIME	FOOD	AMOUNT

sleep schedule

FROM	TO	TOTAL TIME

Activities

baby

Notes

....
....
....
....
....

Shopping list

Diapers

Time	Pee	Poop
......	☐	☐
......	☐	☐
......	☐	☐
......	☐	☐
......	☐	☐
......	☐	☐
......	☐	☐
......	☐	☐

Baby Log Book   Date

eat schedule

TIME	FOOD	AMOUNT

sleep schedule

FROM	TO	TOTAL TIME

Activities

baby

Notes

Diapers

Time	Pee	Poop
……	☐	☐
……	☐	☐
……	☐	☐
……	☐	☐
……	☐	☐
……	☐	☐
……	☐	☐
……	☐	☐

Shopping list

Baby Log Book

Date

eat schedule

TIME	FOOD	AMOUNT

sleep schedule

FROM	TO	TOTAL TIME

Activities

baby

Notes

....
....
....
....
....

Shopping list

Diapers

Time	Pee	Poop
......	☐	☐
......	☐	☐
......	☐	☐
......	☐	☐
......	☐	☐
......	☐	☐
......	☐	☐
......	☐	☐

Baby Log Book   Date

eat schedule

TIME	FOOD	AMOUNT

sleep schedule

FROM	TO	TOTAL TIME

Activities

baby

Notes

....
....
....
....
....

Diapers

Time	Pee	Poop
......	☐	☐
......	☐	☐
......	☐	☐
......	☐	☐
......	☐	☐
......	☐	☐
......	☐	☐
......	☐	☐

Shopping list

Baby Log Book — Date

eat schedule

TIME	FOOD	AMOUNT

sleep schedule

FROM	TO	TOTAL TIME

Activities

baby

Notes

....
....
....
....
....

Shopping list

Diapers

Time	Pee	Poop
......	☐	☐
......	☐	☐
......	☐	☐
......	☐	☐
......	☐	☐
......	☐	☐
......	☐	☐
......	☐	☐

Baby Log Book — Date

eat schedule

TIME	FOOD	AMOUNT

sleep schedule

FROM	TO	TOTAL TIME

Activities

baby

Notes

....
....
....
....
....

Shopping list

Diapers

Time	Pee	Poop
.....	☐	☐
.....	☐	☐
.....	☐	☐
.....	☐	☐
.....	☐	☐
.....	☐	☐
.....	☐	☐
.....	☐	☐

Baby Log Book   Date

eat schedule

TIME	FOOD	AMOUNT

sleep schedule

FROM	TO	TOTAL TIME

Activities

baby

Notes

....
....
....
....
....

Shopping list

Diapers

Time	Pee	Poop
………	☐	☐
………	☐	☐
………	☐	☐
………	☐	☐
………	☐	☐
………	☐	☐
………	☐	☐
………	☐	☐

Baby Log Book   Date

eat schedule

TIME	FOOD	AMOUNT

sleep schedule

FROM	TO	TOTAL TIME

Activities

baby

Notes

....
....
....
....
....

Shopping list

Diapers

Time	Pee	Poop
......	☐	☐
......	☐	☐
......	☐	☐
......	☐	☐
......	☐	☐
......	☐	☐
......	☐	☐
......	☐	☐

Baby Log Book   Date

eat schedule

TIME	FOOD	AMOUNT

sleep schedule

FROM	TO	TOTAL TIME

Activities

baby

Notes

....
....
....
....
....

Shopping list

Diapers

Time	Pee	Poop
.....	☐	☐
.....	☐	☐
.....	☐	☐
.....	☐	☐
.....	☐	☐
.....	☐	☐
.....	☐	☐
.....	☐	☐

Baby Log Book

Date

eat schedule

TIME	FOOD	AMOUNT

sleep schedule

FROM	TO	TOTAL TIME

Activities

baby

Notes

....
....
....
....
....

Shopping list

Diapers

Time	Pee	Poop
......	☐	☐
......	☐	☐
......	☐	☐
......	☐	☐
......	☐	☐
......	☐	☐
......	☐	☐
......	☐	☐

Baby Log Book Date

eat schedule

TIME	FOOD	AMOUNT

sleep schedule

FROM	TO	TOTAL TIME

Activities

baby

Notes

....
....
....
....
....

Shopping list

Diapers

Time	Pee	Poop
.....	☐	☐
.....	☐	☐
.....	☐	☐
.....	☐	☐
.....	☐	☐
.....	☐	☐
.....	☐	☐
.....	☐	☐

Baby Log Book Date

eat schedule

TIME	FOOD	AMOUNT

sleep schedule

FROM	TO	TOTAL TIME

Activities

baby

Notes

....
....
....
....
....

Shopping list

Diapers

Time	Pee	Poop
......	☐	☐
......	☐	☐
......	☐	☐
......	☐	☐
......	☐	☐
......	☐	☐
......	☐	☐
......	☐	☐

Baby Log Book — Date

eat schedule

TIME	FOOD	AMOUNT

sleep schedule

FROM	TO	TOTAL TIME

Activities

baby

Notes

....
....
....
....

Shopping list

Diapers

Time	Pee	Poop
......	☐	☐
......	☐	☐
......	☐	☐
......	☐	☐
......	☐	☐
......	☐	☐
......	☐	☐
......	☐	☐

Baby Log Book   Date

eat schedule

TIME	FOOD	AMOUNT

sleep schedule

FROM	TO	TOTAL TIME

Activities

baby

Notes

....
....
....
....
....

Shopping list

Diapers

Time	Pee	Poop
......	☐	☐
......	☐	☐
......	☐	☐
......	☐	☐
......	☐	☐
......	☐	☐
......	☐	☐
......	☐	☐

Baby Log Book   Date

eat schedule

TIME	FOOD	AMOUNT

sleep schedule

FROM	TO	TOTAL TIME

Activities

baby

Notes

....
....
....
....
....

Shopping list

Diapers

Time	Pee	Poop
......	☐	☐
......	☐	☐
......	☐	☐
......	☐	☐
......	☐	☐
......	☐	☐
......	☐	☐
......	☐	☐

Baby Log Book   Date

eat schedule

TIME	FOOD	AMOUNT

sleep schedule

FROM	TO	TOTAL TIME

Activities

baby

Notes

....
....
....
....
....

Shopping list

Diapers

Time	Pee	Poop
......	☐	☐
......	☐	☐
......	☐	☐
......	☐	☐
......	☐	☐
......	☐	☐
......	☐	☐
......	☐	☐

Baby Log Book Date

eat schedule

TIME	FOOD	AMOUNT

sleep schedule

FROM	TO	TOTAL TIME

Activities

baby

Notes

....
....
....
....
....

Diapers

Time	Pee	Poop
....	☐	☐
....	☐	☐
....	☐	☐
....	☐	☐
....	☐	☐
....	☐	☐
....	☐	☐
....	☐	☐

Shopping list

Baby Log Book — Date

eat schedule

TIME	FOOD	AMOUNT

sleep schedule

FROM	TO	TOTAL TIME

Activities

baby

Notes

....
....
....
....
....

Shopping list

Diapers

Time	Pee	Poop
………	☐	☐
………	☐	☐
………	☐	☐
………	☐	☐
………	☐	☐
………	☐	☐
………	☐	☐
………	☐	☐

Baby Log Book   Date

eat schedule

TIME	FOOD	AMOUNT

sleep schedule

FROM	TO	TOTAL TIME

Activities

baby

Notes

....
....
....
....
....

Shopping list

Diapers

Time	Pee	Poop
......	☐	☐
......	☐	☐
......	☐	☐
......	☐	☐
......	☐	☐
......	☐	☐
......	☐	☐
......	☐	☐

Baby Log Book Date

eat schedule

TIME	FOOD	AMOUNT

sleep schedule

FROM	TO	TOTAL TIME

Activities

baby

Notes

....
....
....
....
....

Shopping list

Diapers

Time	Pee	Poop
......	☐	☐
......	☐	☐
......	☐	☐
......	☐	☐
......	☐	☐
......	☐	☐
......	☐	☐
......	☐	☐

Baby Log Book Date

eat schedule

TIME	FOOD	AMOUNT

sleep schedule

FROM	TO	TOTAL TIME

Activities

baby

Notes

....
....
....
....
....

Shopping list

Diapers

Time	Pee	Poop
....	☐	☐
....	☐	☐
....	☐	☐
....	☐	☐
....	☐	☐
....	☐	☐
....	☐	☐
....	☐	☐

Baby Log Book

Date

eat schedule

TIME	FOOD	AMOUNT

sleep schedule

FROM	TO	TOTAL TIME

Activities

baby

Notes

....
....
....
....
....

Shopping list

Diapers

Time	Pee	Poop
......	☐	☐
......	☐	☐
......	☐	☐
......	☐	☐
......	☐	☐
......	☐	☐
......	☐	☐
......	☐	☐

Baby Log Book Date

eat schedule

TIME	FOOD	AMOUNT

sleep schedule

FROM	TO	TOTAL TIME

Activities

baby

Notes

Diapers

Time	Pee	Poop
......	☐	☐
......	☐	☐
......	☐	☐
......	☐	☐
......	☐	☐
......	☐	☐
......	☐	☐
......	☐	☐

Shopping list

Baby Log Book

Date

eat schedule

TIME	FOOD	AMOUNT

sleep schedule

FROM	TO	TOTAL TIME

Activities

baby

Notes

....
....
....
....
....

Shopping list

Diapers

Time	Pee	Poop
......	☐	☐
......	☐	☐
......	☐	☐
......	☐	☐
......	☐	☐
......	☐	☐
......	☐	☐
......	☐	☐

Baby Log Book   Date

eat schedule

TIME	FOOD	AMOUNT

sleep schedule

FROM	TO	TOTAL TIME

Activities

baby

Notes

....
....
....
....
....

Shopping list

Diapers

Time	Pee	Poop
.....	☐	☐
.....	☐	☐
.....	☐	☐
.....	☐	☐
.....	☐	☐
.....	☐	☐
.....	☐	☐
.....	☐	☐

Baby Log Book

Date

eat schedule

TIME	FOOD	AMOUNT

sleep schedule

FROM	TO	TOTAL TIME

Activities

baby

Notes

....
....
....
....
....

Shopping list

Diapers

Time	Pee	Poop
......	☐	☐
......	☐	☐
......	☐	☐
......	☐	☐
......	☐	☐
......	☐	☐
......	☐	☐
......	☐	☐

Baby Log Book

Date

eat schedule

TIME	FOOD	AMOUNT

sleep schedule

FROM	TO	TOTAL TIME

Activities

baby

Notes

....
....
....
....
....

Shopping list

Diapers

Time	Pee	Poop
......	☐	☐
......	☐	☐
......	☐	☐
......	☐	☐
......	☐	☐
......	☐	☐
......	☐	☐
......	☐	☐

Baby Log Book

Date

eat schedule

TIME	FOOD	AMOUNT

sleep schedule

FROM	TO	TOTAL TIME

Activities

baby

Notes

....
....
....
....
....

Shopping list

Diapers

Time	Pee	Poop
....	☐	☐
....	☐	☐
....	☐	☐
....	☐	☐
....	☐	☐
....	☐	☐
....	☐	☐
....	☐	☐

Baby Log Book   Date

eat schedule

TIME	FOOD	AMOUNT

sleep schedule

FROM	TO	TOTAL TIME

Activities

baby

Notes

....
....
....
....
....

Shopping list

Diapers

Time	Pee	Poop
......	☐	☐
......	☐	☐
......	☐	☐
......	☐	☐
......	☐	☐
......	☐	☐
......	☐	☐
......	☐	☐

Baby Log Book

Date

eat schedule

TIME	FOOD	AMOUNT

sleep schedule

FROM	TO	TOTAL TIME

Activities

baby

Notes

....
....
....
....
....

Shopping list

Diapers

Time	Pee	Poop
......	☐	☐
......	☐	☐
......	☐	☐
......	☐	☐
......	☐	☐
......	☐	☐
......	☐	☐
......	☐	☐

www.ingramcontent.com/pod-product-compliance
Lightning Source LLC
LaVergne TN
LVHW060141080526
838202LV00049B/4042